IOWA THE TALL

By Mary Wilcox

an *EXECU-CRAFTS* book

Published by
COLLISON AGENCY
26 — 12th S.E.
Mason City, Iowa

Printed in the U.S.A. by
Graphic Publishing Co., Inc.
Lake Mills, Iowa

DEDICATION
TO THE MOTHER OF GOOD HARVEST

INTRODUCTION

"Our Lord built our Land tall"

And the tallness lay hidden for centuries under prairie sod. In a new age scientists and geologists probe deep into the innards of the land, stretch wide the horizon of the mind . . . and discover what a crippled boy in Mason City, Iowa, knew poetically:

Eddie Hodnefeld—crippled since birth, unable to speak or use his hands—"told" the author of this book, "I've never seen the Rocky Mountains. But I don't have to. Iowa has her own Rocky Mountains—under the earth!"

Eddie can't talk, he can't write, he can't stand, he can't walk. Hidden in his frail and slender body is a brilliant mind. "Though Eddie cannot support himself physically nor stretch to full height," Mary Wilcox tells former President Hoover in her Open Letter, "he stands tall as the independent tradition of Iowa."

Iowa's wealth of soil and mineral stands taller than the Rocky Mountains! Her wealth of mind and spirit stands taller than the fame of her football teams and her harvested corn.

Iowa's tall men tower, to reach the height of the vital power of our land.

Iowa is Tall.

CONTENTS

Iowa Speaks .... page 1

Open Letter to President Hoover 9

Famous Persons Visit Iowa 20

Poem Portraits 33

Sing Iowa 51

CHAPTER I

IOWA SPEAKS

I

IOWA SPEAKS

(To my Father, whose enduring, quiet strength in everyday living images to me the faith, hope and love inherent in Tall Men.)

Iowa called to Brother Wind,
"Come, sweep my streets and prairie earth
And stir the air.
And blow your gusty self into my soul,
Inflame my pride, unfurl it wide—
Oh, Brother Wind, come be my pulse!
Tease my tawny fingers with your breath to sway my
      height;
Then fill the depth and breadth of me with life—
Loud and lusty, city cadence sound,
Field-talking, quiet power tone,
Canticles of progress, lipped by tall men—

Heavy light-time voice————but
When silhouette is purple-tinged and hazy,
Harp a lullaby that I may learn
The splendid variation of your song.
I listen to the harmony of earth and I am soothed
But never lulled to sleep.
How could I dare to slumber in this vital stage of man?
Or catnap? That alone is luxury————
Too dear at any price!
I *cannot* sleep,
For I, Centrifugal Force of Harvest Might,
Am busy growing stature—silent strength—
For all the world to emulate my strength.
Your Iowa is tall, O Brother Wind,
And growing taller,
     dreaming wider
         building stronger————
I flex my muscles dawn to dawn
And manufacture means to serve humanity.
My bounty is the weapon of a world loving Freedom:
A challenge for a country to uphold.
And I know the mincing Menace
Of the Fox who pawed my prairie
Is lusting my abundance from his den;
So my heart is pounding faster,
But my limbs are looming longer
And my back is broader, stronger
Than it ever was before!
I'm gigantic compilation
Of a vast, productive network
Of family and commercial factory.
The industry of soil————and seed————and reaping
Run by Dynamo of God and Sun.
I'm a Giant with a cornstalk in my hand—

A beanstock that could blast around the world—
While you and I are welded to the steel,
Mortared to the concrete and the brick,
Rooted to the earth that *is* America.
I *am* America!
Oh, Spirit-Kin, we move as one
In sheer velocity.
Vibrant, volar, vascular Wind-Voice,
You are my voice!
So howl or damn or bless me as you will—
But blow
And suck the earth to my embrace."

Iowa then exhorted Wind,
"Go, tell the world that I want men
Of quiet strength to toil me
And grow me tall
And through my universities to learn of me
And grow me wise
To plant and plow and fertilize the mind
And so the physical as well
And underneath
To reap the rocky mountain innards of my wealth."

Iowa cried again———again,
"Come, take my precious produce
And dispense it to our nation,
Give my golden, good life substance
Of the earth's fertility
Of my own abundant prairies
And their might of industry.
I, the Breadland of the Nation,
From the Midwest Prairie Portals
Help to share the health of Freedom with all lands—

While you, the Wind,
And I, your Brother Iowa,
Dynamos of Progress ,
Join hands."

CHAPTER II

OPEN LETTER TO PRESIDENT HOOVER

pathy, when it was self-imposed at the sight of class-mate David Wilson rounding the corner at the far end of the corridor *behind* his wheel chair instead of *in* it?

The fragileness of the boy's slight, struggling frame was emphasized by the presence of the tall, energetic man at his side. David was being accompanied to his classroom by his friend, physical therapist William D. Otterman. Not a word was spoken by any one of David's fellow students, albeit there were tears in the eyes of some—of the boys as well as the girls—while boy, man and wheel chair advanced down the hall to the fourth grade room. They were followed by an awed procession of nine and ten-year-olds, David's devoted friends, who apparently were as happy and as thankful for his accomplishment as they could have been for an own brother.

Quietly they filed into their classroom and watched Mr. Otterman lift David into his accustomed seat in the wheel chair, a wheel chair which the small owner had so valiantly navigated (only moments before) down a corridor hushed in almost reverent silence—past viewers who were keenly perceptive. These children were not strangers to compassion.

In visiting the Herbert Hoover Elementary School here in Mason City, Iowa, the marvels that I witnessed in the classrooms, along the corridors, on the play-ground, and in the therapy room connected with the school have impelled me to write and share these wonders with you, our former President, the man who dedicated this educational structure. Located in the heart of the richest agricultural region in the world, this institution of learning is producing an aura of spirit as fruitful as the Iowa soil on which it is founded. Even as an abundant crop is the goodness of Providence to the farmer in this your home state so, too, you will be pleased to know that Herbert Hoover Elementary School, over and above everything else, is the answer to a very strong need in our community————God's answer to every mother and father in this area who have a seriously crippled child.

According to S. Bernie Waldon, Director of Special Education Services for Mason City Public Schools, there are many, if not more, services for handicapped children in Hoover School in Mason City than in any other regular school in the state. Although it is a typical three-unit school with the standard curriculum, this institution of elementary learning is unique in that it has an extended program to meet the demands and the needs of those children who require special education.

Basic concepts of humanism are an intangible factor of this uniqueness. The spirit of compassion cannot be *seen*. It is *felt*. It is manifested through humanitarian impulses. It can be most eloquent in silence.

Boys and girls, who grow up in a school with handicapped children, will understand them, and understanding, they will overcome that almost inborn adversion to those who are physically different from themselves. As for the crippled children, they have the opportunity of day by day contact with youngsters not physically handicapped, who accept them—who *want* them as playmates. At Hoover School, the handicapped boys and girls are accepted as normal children, because they go along with normal children. And so they build a satisfactory feeling of personal worth.

According to Mr. Otterman, registered physical therapist and executive director of the Cerro Gordo County Easter Seal Society, a handicap is a matter of degree. "In some ways we are all handicapped," he contends.

A handicap is a *handicap* only so long as it prevents us from doing some specific job. The worse handicap is in the mind—it is really a state of mind." In referring to the crippled children under his charge, he explains, "Their attitude toward themselves is basic. We shape these attitudes. That is just as important as any other treatment."

Crippled children in the Mason City area have the advantage of participating in the regular school curriculum, while under the same roof they also can receive physical therapy treatments. Mr. Hoover, possibly you remember being conducted through the room, which was to serve this purpose, when you were here to dedicate the school August 11th, 1953. Two months after your visit to Mason City, physical therapy service was inaugurated in the educational structure which bears your name with a unique Easter Seal Society-school system tie-up. This was the first program in Iowa—your state and mine—operated jointly by school and Society.

It was here that the parents of Walter Bill Cash, the 1957 Easter Seal Child, found the highly specialized services which have lifted their son from dependency and placed him on his own two feet and active life commensurate with the vivacity of his nature. This was the only care of its kind within a hundred-mile radius of the Cash farm home at Clear Lake, Iowa. As long as extensive treatment was necessary a cheerful boy and a grateful mother commuted ten miles three times a week to the Easter Seal center housed in Herbert Hoover School. And though Walter Bill was not enrolled in the school, his valiant spirit has left a mark. Such a vital personality as his in constant association with 25 children, patient-pupils, was bound to engender moral intercom between therapy wing and classrooms. Moreover, while I can cite many courageous counterparts of Walter Bill, I mention him in particular, because as the 1957 Easter Seal Child he drew national distinction to the Cerro Gordo County Easter Seal center, that is linked inseparably with the Hoover School. Each is an integral part of a whole, symbolized in 1957 to the United States of America by one small, Iowa boy. Tiny crutches cast long shadows————

Many are the crutches and wheel chairs that have hallowed the halls of "Hoover" over the past decade of its existence. One teacher comments, "I have never yet taught in this school when I did not have a wheel chair case." What the crippled children of Herbert Hoover School do not harvest themselves in the way of exploring outer space or building bigger and better empires on earth, the "unhandicapped" children, whom they have touched, may very well accomplish *because of them.* For they have been exposed to excellent climatic conditions of cultivation.

Mr. Hoover, if you were to revisit your namesake structure in Mason City, you would be certain to hear about Eddie Hodnefield, the young author who can neither speak nor write nor walk. He has practically no control over his muscles, having suffered from birth from athetoid cerebral palsy. But the frail body houses an indomitable spirit.

Though Eddie cannot support himself physically nor stretch to full height, he stands tall as the independent tradition of Iowa.

The heritage of the land is his and he builds his world with a state of mind equivalent to the same perseverance and faith of those who live and work in close relationship with nourishing soil. Eddie's family, the John

13

Hodnefields, operated a 126-acre grain and stock farm near Scarville, Iowa, until the boy was fifteen years of age. Then, like many other parents in the North Iowa area, they uprooted the family and moved to Mason City, so that Eddie could have the opportunity of formal education.

Although for two years Eddie previously had attended a school for handicapped children at Lake Mills, his enrollment at Herbert Hoover Elementary School marked the beginning of a new, exciting life for him. Concerning his attitude of the school venture, his mother once declared, "Eddie likes school so much we can hardly keep him at home. He even wants to go to school when he's sick."

By the same token, Eddie was a memorable experience for the school, because this boy is a unique human being. Meeting Eddie is a soul-searing event. His keen, blue eyes spark communication without speech. His smile is infectious. His interest in you is immediate, sincere, obvious, and flattering. He loves the world and is loved back in proportion to his giving.

He was beloved by the children in the sixth grade class at Hoover School. He was accepted—he was liked —he was loved—he was courted. The other children vied for his favor. They got to fighting for the privilege of caring for him: wheeling him to the therapy room and back to the classroom; wiping his mouth; getting his books and so forth. Peacemaker Eddie compiled a list and systematically made the appointments for a specified time. In this way, each child had a "turn." Eddie said, "I had to fire one boy, because he didn't take care of his responsibilities."

As an indication of the "fellows" regard for Eddie, I quote one of his classmates, Tod Ettner, "You know,

14

before Eddie started writing poetry, I thought it was 'sissy stuff'." Who knows, Mr. Hoover, maybe one or more of the sixth graders of Eddie's class may bring literary fame to Iowa—because they respected and loved a boy in a wheel chair.

As for *Eddie's* poetry, it is far from "sissy stuff." It is about the earth and people and faith in God. Eddie's independent nature is fortified by a deep dependence on God, and so he writes.

Considering the laborious method of communication with which he must contend, the fact that he can create a poem at all is considered a remarkable feat.

Eddie works with an alphabet list divided into five sections. The person working with him points to each list. Eddie indicates "yes" when the helper comes to the list which contains the letter Eddie wants. Then the helper goes through the letters in that list until Eddie indicates "yes" for the right letter.

He is able to shake his head to indicate "no" and lifts his left arm to indicate "yes." This is Eddie's way of "speaking."

Another child at another time asked a question. This question he directed to his mother is one that I suppose is asked by *all* crippled children. "Why do you suppose that God made me crippled?"

One mother gave her little boy this answer, "You have a good mind and your handicap may be the door for opportunity—for developing your mind. *Because* of your disability your mind will reach out to greater heights. You will grow as tall and stand as high as any man."

I told Eddie I was writing to you about the school he attended and he came up with the following poem:

15

"MEMORIES OF HOOVER SCHOOL"

The school was named for Herbert Hoover, to which I
    went to learn
Reading, writing and arithmetic. And some day I hope
    to return
To meet the people whom I once knew and whom I
    made my friends,
The teachers and janitors and many more—the list just
    never ends!
So if you ever drive through "River City"—and we'll be
    honored if you do—
You are welcome to look over
        the school that I went to.

And the 400 youngsters each year, who accept these crippled children as individuals—as David or Eddie—on the basis of individual talents and abilities, are growing tall—are reaching out beyond themselves. In everyday play. In helpful assistance *only when needed*. In casual tit for tat "on the same level" treatment. In the annual student-initiated talent show project, "The Hoover School Varieties," performed for student body and evening adult audience to raise money which will help their crippled classmates. In feeling pride and personal satisfaction—in cheering—the physical or scholastic accomplishments of their visibly handicapped friends.

Such is the crop of future citizens of our community that is being nurtured in the heart of the wealthiest agricultural and industrial region in the world—in the educational structure that bears your name, the Herbert Hoover Elementary School of Mason City, Iowa. It is appropriate that this unique embodiment of learning and compassionate endeavor bears the name of our country's most beloved humanitarian.

Respectfully,
Mary Wilcox

III

FAMOUS PERSONS
VISIT IOWA

ART LINKLETTER SAID

"I don't feel at all unfamiliar in these surroundings, because, strange to say, I'm a farmer, too—part time," declared Art Linkletter, seated in the lobby of the Roosevelt Hotel in Cedar Rapids, Iowa. Daughter Mary Leeann and I had just introduced ourselves as Mason Cityans. And setting up my tape recorder for an impromptu interview, I handed the mike to the genial host of television's "House Party."

Having been informed that Art Linkletter would be staying over in Cedar Rapids after his appearance at the National Cattle Congress in Waterloo, I had suggested a switch of route. An interview with this famous man for my show over Radio Station KSMN had been my aim. The family had no objections so there I was in Cedar Rapids interviewing the man who usually did the interviewing.

Our early morning motor trip through the autumnal countryside had exposed the splendor and fulfillment of the season in a setting we had failed to explore previously. So far the outing had been a success—from a family viewpoint—and with my pride of Iowa newly exhilarated, I was anxious to know what a world-traveler thought about our state.

"Have you ever been to the National Cattle Congress before?" was my query.

"Never before. This is the first time, although I've owned Angus herds and been interested in cattle shows in other parts of the country."

"Does being here at the National Cattle Congress give you an idea of what the state of Iowa is like?" I pursued.

"Well, I've always been very appreciative of the richness and vast variety of farm products of which Iowa is proud," Mr. Linkletter reflected. "But," he continued, "the cows that I've seen here are just about as good as I've ever seen in any part of the world. I was very much impressed by the prices some of them brought and also the general variety of the dairy herds shown."

Mr. Linkletter contends we should be proud of our agricultural economy. "It's the basis of wealth for any country," he declared during the Cedar Rapids interview.

SAM LEVENSON

Educator . . . Parent . . . Humanitarian

"Do you want to start with me? I'm the proverbial poor kid!" declared Sam Levenson as he visited with me at the 1962 Iowa State Education Association convention in Des Moines, Iowa. Notwithstanding the pressure of the moment, the kindly gentleman had generously accorded me time for a personal interview and I had asked,

—"Do you think there is a difference between rural and urban children?" I inquired.

"There is," he shot back and repeated, "there is. I might surprise you," he ventured. "You might think I would say the big city is the place to raise children. It isn't necessarily so at all."

He explained, "When you say rural, you have to know *what* rural. Your rural out here is good. I have noticed here—and I've been through cities in the entire midwest area—there is a great cleanliness about your people out here. They are a *clean* people. They are thrifty people and this is healthy. They have somehow retained a certain amount of the pioneer spirit about them that I find very good. They are not wasteful. When they eat, they eat everything! I notice they clean off the plate, while in New York, they'll buy a dinner with languor, take a nibble and then throw the rest away. I've seen a lot of them that way and I think it's utterly wrong." At this point in our discussion, Mr. Levenson, the humanitarian, was very grave. "You see," he continued, "if you're talking about which I respect more as civilization—I respect these people that have simple values much more than so-called sophistication in a big city."

I had heard that his parents had rural backgrounds and asked Mr. Levenson if this were true.

"My parents were peasants," he replied. "They came from Russia—from very small towns, so that what I was raised in actually was a small town in a big city."

"New York," he continued, "is a big noisy, dirty city, but my mother was raised like poor farm folk were raised and we *never wasted anything!*" Again, Mr. Levenson emphasized every syllable by thumping the table with his fingers. He went on to explain, "She had a sense of the intelligent use of time. She was always mending, always patching. There was work to be done and boys helped around the house just as girls helped around the house. So you see that essentially I was raised on a farm—except that it was in a tenement," he smiled.

I suggested to Mr. Levenson that with such a background he should feel right at home in Iowa and extended him a welcome.

"Thank you," he responded graciously. "I feel very much at home."

"What do you think of rural-urban exchange for our young people? Do you think it would help to clear up some of our legislative problems if we could educate our future leaders by a rural-urban exchange? What do you think would grow out of this?" I questioned.

"Well," Mr. Levenson said thoughtfully, "the boy from the city could certainly use the country environment. And I think that a boy living in a big city like New York, coming from a small town or a farm would perhaps understand the problems of the city boy and be much more sympathetic to him. I find wherever I go people think that in New York or a big city like that everything is wrong and the kids are all juvenile delinquents.

"It isn't so to begin with," he spoke with conviction and the humanitarian nature of the man was apparent as he continued in a more gentle tone. "I want to preach a slight sermon in favor of that kid. We have migrant kids in New York, you see, that have no stability—no roots—no tradition. Out here, there's a farmhouse that's been standing for 100 years and some of them have been in the same family for generations. That's stability—that's roots. In New York very few people have roots of that kind."

"Of course, we have many things that your kids don't have. Around the corner from almost any community in New York there are big libraries and big theaters and fine museums and there are children's concerts. There are many things that we have that you don't have in the same amount, but we should trade in these things," Mr. Levenson advised. "And the kids in New York could gather a little bit of your sunshine and color and soil in their shoes. It would do them a world of good."

BACKSTAGE AT THE
IOWA STATE FAIR . . . 1963

Sitting in a deserted dressing room backstage at the Iowa State Fair in Des Moines, I held in my hand a size 12 shoe—belonging to none other than Buster Keaton. All the dressing rooms were deserted, but this one had a special fascination for me because here were the trademarks of a man who was vaudeville tradition. The flat hat—or pork pie—and the size 12s!

Hoping to get some good interviews, I moved out to the hall to visit with Sam Levy, producer of Barnes and Corruthers, the company presenting the night grandstand show. Mr. and Mrs. Levy were seated on chairs at the bottom of a flight of stairs leading up to the pit. The stock car races were in progress and the sound of the motors exploded about us. Mr. Levy introduced me to his wife, a small, kindly woman, who at the moment was concerned over the welfare of the drivers. There had been one or two accidents, but, so far, no one had been injured that afternoon.

As we were visiting, Ken Fulk, State Fair secretary, joined us and we all got around to discussing the merits of the county fair.

"If we didn't have the county fairs, we wouldn't have 4-H or FFA," remarked Mrs. Levy.

"You've got to have motivation to get these kids doing things," added Ken Fulk.

"City people should support the county fair," interjected Sam Levy. "The county fair's a good way to bring business into the town."

His son, Sam, Jr., manager of the show—busy with many details of preparation for the night performance—stopped by to confer with his father. Hearing the comments, he gave his opinion as to the business value of the fair. "The better the fair, the more people will come to visit; the more people who visit, the better for business." He cited the Harvet Festival at Fort Dodge as a fine example.

My original purpose in visiting backstage was to arrange an interview with the special guest star, Rosemary Clooney. Sam, Jr., advised me to come back later that evening and he assured me Miss Clooney would visit with me then as would many of the other performers.

Earlier in the year I had interviewed Ken Fulk for my radio show in Mason City. We had discussed the fact that the Iowa State Fair should be considered an industry in and of itself—"a tall one at that," I mused that evening as I headed backstage.

Buster Keaton was in costume—replete with pork pie and the "big feet" shoes. I was thrilled at the opportunity of visiting with a man whom I had always considered a really great entertainer.

I asked, "What image do you have of Iowa?"

The entertainer, whose mother had been born in Council Bluffs, Iowa replied, "Oh, I know it's a great state! It's the top agricultural state of the union. This is a new experience to be playing these fairs. This one here in Des Moines is the second one I've been in. This is a honey here—this is a pip!" declared the "dead pan" pantomime king.

"Do you think city people should take an interest in them?"

"Sure they should," he declared.

"Why?" I queried.

"We ought to know more about this type of state— that's why! It would help us to appreciate agriculture," he explained and excused himself to make ready for his act.

26

A tall, handsome man approached me and introduced himself as Nip Nelson. I recognized a face that I had seen on Ed Sullivan's TV variety show on several occasions and I was flattered when he congratulated me on writing *Iowa the Tall*.

And he remarked that Iowa audiences were really TALL!

Such a pleasure to meet a native Iowan with the show! Charles Carman, featured as a part of the Appleton act, was born and raised in Buffalo Center. His brother is G. A. Carman, Mayor of Buffalo Center, who has the Buffalo Center *Tribune* and the Lakota newspaper. Charles Carman has appeared an CBS and NBC TV and in the movies.

In answer to my question, "Is there a difference in the audiences in the Midwest from those in other parts of the country?" he replied, "It depends upon the physical set-up. You get better reaction if the stage is closer to the people. The State Fair here has improved its physical set-up 100%," he observed.

Just then Sam Levy, Jr., informed me that Miss Clooney was in her dressing room and was ready for the recorded interview.

I found Rosemary Clooney to be a lovely, gracious woman, even more beautiful off-screen than on. And here is a transcription of the recording:

Question: "Rosemary, can you tell the difference between a farm and a city woman?"

Answer: "I would say no. I was brought up in a very small town in Kentucky. My family were brought up on farms surrounding there. Ohio, too, is an agricultural state, as you know, and I came from that part of the country. I think there is very little difference at all."

Question: "Rosemary, do you think that there is a certain amount of sincerity among farm people that you don't find in big cities or do you think that sincerity is an individual thing?"

Answer: "I think it has entirely to do with the individual, Mary. I don't think that one would be more sincere than the other. I think you will find just as many sincere people inside the city limits as outside. I think that perhaps persons that live on a farm, who subsist on what they grow and just sort of provide for themselves are much more self-contained. Perhaps they don't have the frenetic approach to living that city life has forced on many people that live in crowded cities today."

Question: "Do you think that the average city person realizes how very much he is dependent upon agriculture for the economy of his community?"

Answer: "I think perhaps many individuals do not realize how much they are dependent upon the farmer as the mainstay of their existence. I would say that these people who do not realize it though, Mary, are in the minority. I think that most of the people do."

Question: "Do you think that there is any way that farm and city people could draw closer together in understanding?"

Answer: "I think these state fairs have a lot to do with bringing farm and city people closer together."

Question: "Do you think that mothers like yourself and like me can do anything through their children to promote better understanding between the various segments of our population?"

Answer: "I'm trying myself as I know you are, because you're aware of it. I think that mothers could, if they were made more aware of the importance of it. I think that mothers could do a great deal—yes."

CHAPTER IV

POEM PORTRAITS

MARIAN ANDERSON

IV

POEM PORTRAITS

PORTRAIT OF MANKIND

(A Tribute to Marian Anderson)

A mighty Hand with pallette poised
From genesis of time
Stroked with perfect mastery
Figures of mortality
Upon the universe:
Dark velvet,
Diadem the night—let heaven speak,
While starlit windows of the firmament
Contrast the light-flood noon.
White of day—varied hues of whiteness
Pale into eve;
But not without a glory-burst of yellow fusion,
Coalescing night and day
The Master's way.

A mighty Hand with palette poised
On canvas of our time
Sketched a lark of artistry,
Symbol of equality,
To live for all minorities
The world wide!
Dark velvet,
May the winged lark of song
Bear strains
Of Schubert, Bach, and Brahms and Wolf
And spirituals of faith
To heaven's glowing height

And sound among the stars that arch the universe;
To soar infinity
Where angels fuse their choirs with the lark:
Ave Maria voiced,

Unbounded benediction.
Tranquil, soft, electric, vibrant, rich and vital
Deep-night velvet,
Mind-challenging, line-searing, star-fired essence,
Echoing to earth,
Parallel
With white-flood noon
And glory-burst of yellow sunset.

In the Master's composition
Man is brother to his brother;
Black and white and yellow blend
To complement each other.

A mighty Hand with palette poised
From genesis of time
Planned a perfect symphony of multi-hue,
Harmony of man.

IOWA *IS* INDUSTRY

(Dedicated to George Foerstner, president of Amana Refrigeration, Inc. . . . and to
all Iowa industrialists who join each day in "spreading wide the fame of Iowan skill.")

Amana's industry is tall,
A living plant of modern progeny,
Rising high and spreading wide the fame of Iowan skill.
Sprawling like an athlete
Crouched to leap with agile prowess
Record footage,
The factory looms its might above millrace,
Old component stream of pioneer tradition
Now obscured by giant, growing strength.
A busy smokestack puffs and furls
Charcoal wreaths of productivity—
Man-made
Promise-plumes of manufactured wealth;
While nearby cattle low in meadowland
And banquet nature's bounty.

Industry is labor stretching tall
So Iowa is tall and casting wide.
City, town and village know its height!

And in Amana's Middle Colony
Honest bone and sinew of a state
Pump new ideas and shiny products of precision,
Prairie-built,
To sister states and through the nation,
Powered by the muscle of its men
That tower tall and straight,
Seeding white-heat root
In green and cool pasture.

Iowa sons are tall
And in Amana
There is one of vim, efficient vein, of ingenuity,
Tall of stature,
Steel-forged on international horizons.
Exotic trademarks shout democracy,
Amana-giving know-how to the world.
Loyal purpose bent the bow of that Amana son
Aiming true for progress of his own community;
Reflecting all such leaders of a land
Who pioneered with modest practicality.

These vibrant salesmen of state
Plant human manufactories of might,
Drive girders deep in prairie earth,
Reap the power, the talent of tall men
Who pitch their song of progress through the state,
Sounding out the saga of production:
Humming, drilling, buzzing—
Blending with the canticle of creatures
Of an ever-teeming land
And the whooing of the wind through branching oak.
And all of these go hand in hand
Where farm and factory
Are pulsing, prudent partners of the plain.

Smokestacks punctuate the scene
And fling a friendly arm around God's acres:
Tall in harvest-glory of the seed,
Tall in many-varied crops of man-made skill.

Industry, diversified and Iowa-bred,
Is manned by drivers disciplined to labor,
Tall and stable men attuned to growth.

TALL WOMANHOOD

Champion, challenger, mentor of might,
Womanhood images Iowa's role!
Meeting the needs of the world is her goal,
Where and whenever a woman can cite
Attributes worthy for serving the right
Policy making position. To scroll
Womanhood power and beauty of soul,
Business, professional prowess and height
Glorifies Iowa history made.
History still in the making will chart
Progress in partnership—full, unafraid.
Learned, responsible, primed for the part,
Qualified women accept and upgrade
Leadership wrought of patience and art.

IOWAN FARMER-PRODUCER

(Dedicated to Iowan farmer-producer and agribusiness executive Morel Stientjes, whose life has been one of service to his fellow-farmers and to Iowa's gigantic agricultural industry. His philosophy was the inspiration for this poem.)

Production and marketing expert,
A businessman selling his stock,
He stands for conviction and courage,
Enduring and weathered as rock.

His calling is one to be honored:
He labors with love of the sod—
A man in communion with nature
Who chose to be partner with God.

He knows the contentment of wholeness,
Completing the cycle of growth;
An integral being with purpose
Accorded the earth his betroth.

Responsible citizen, voter,
Taxpayer, neighbor and friend,
Providing our food and our fiber
His knowledge and skill are a blend

Of engineer, chemist, mechanic,
Often a statesman as well;
So walks the farmer-producer
With a harvest no land can excel.

MOTHERHOOD

(To my Mother)

A mother moves in clothesline harness,
motive parallel
to diaper horizons,
rows of bottled formula,
shades of playpen bars.
Her reins are taunt and tattered,
childworn,
until she cradles tiny palm and fingers in her own
and reaches out
to cup eternity.

PEOPLE TO PEOPLE

(Inspired by and dedicated to Murray Lincoln, President of CARE)

Pastoral scenes portray abounding gold:
A nation's food and food of nations spread
On prairie table—basketland of bread,
Of goldstuffs heaped and overflowing, scrolled
On balance sheets in heaven. Seeds unfold
And stalks explode to that celestial stead
From whence the wise Cooperator shed
Such bounty for America to hold.

Abundant scenes portray a sacred trust:
Our farmers tend in partnership with God
The harvest-hope committed to our care.
The earth's emaciated creatures *must*
Be nurtured by the breath of Freedom's sod,
As freemen give and hungry peoples share.

THE WINGED BUILDER

(Inspired by and Dedicated to My Little Friend David, Polio Victim)

The nest cast arms and wheeled-flanks about his feet,
but shadows cannot bind
a fledgling born to fly—
a child spreads his wings!
Wings that lift the spirit from the chair
and raise the fragile body he would build—
wings—invincible, heroic,
brave the endless labor of the body's flight,
fluttering and pain-propelled and weary—still,
wings impel the heart and all the parts of one who
      builds.

And so he builds—
he builds the wasted sinews inch by inch
along the twin expanse of steel bars,
parallel and cold, but promise prone and challenging
to one of such an essence to create,
with vision to design
a boy-dream of ships for outer space;
while silver wings take flight on practice bars.

WINTER ARTISTRY

(Dedicated to the Decorah, Iowa, scenic area)

A gleaming crystal chandelier,
Majestic arm of Norway pine,
Is wafted by a gentle peer
That stirs the arced cathedral shrine.

The colonnade of pillared birch
That tower to a vaulted crest,
Converge to roof a woodland church
Of fir and balsam coalesced.

The wind is harpist of the shrine,
Of fir and balsam coalesced;
When plucked on icy bough or vine,
Her melody is loveliest.

The candelabra domineer
The ceiling of a woodland church,
While on the virgin carpet veer
The winged creatures from their perch.

Candescent arm of Norway pine,
Aglitter from its vaulted crest,
Is threaded in a rare design,
Chantilly lace upon her breast.

Lo, gleam each crystal chandelier!
On colonnade of pillared birch
The candelabra domineer
The glory of a woodland church.

THE P. R. MAN

(Dedicated to a former mayor of Belmond, Iowa.)

He muscles the might of public relations.
A sparkplug of wisdom and wit,
He drives with dynamic and dominant will
And a talent of words to transmit
Company policy, progress and aim,
The future intent of the firm
To the customer. One to personify skill,
As he utters each technical term,
He wields the power of phrasing—a blend
Of business with humor is art;
But the magic of this man's good public relations
Is the humanized brand that has heart.

CHAPTER V

SING IOWA

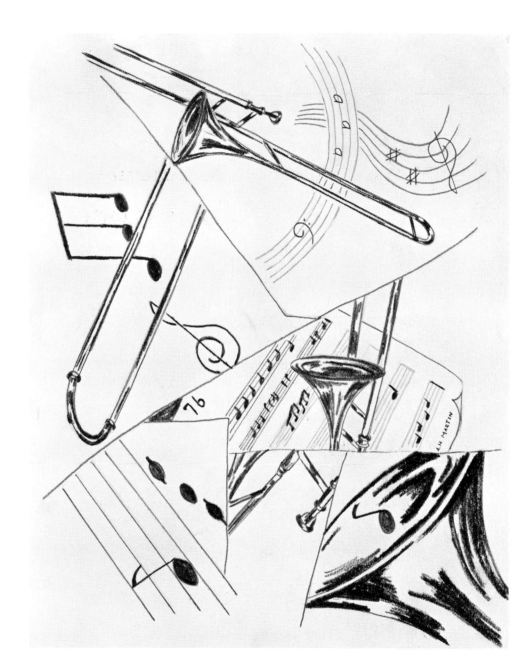

SING IOWA

RIVER CITY—JUNE 19th, 1962

Hear ye! Hear ye! See today
A legend in the making:
Our country's youth is on display
To all the world; their bands convey
The vibrant spirit of our land
And one town's undertaking
And one man's dream awaking
A world of song and laughter and nostalgia he
      created
From memories of that boyhood town
He often contemplated.

Iowa is our nation's heart;
Now hear that heart resounding—
Hear ye! Hear that Iowa beat—
A nation's pulse is pounding!
Bands from thirty states compete,
Complete the twenty-fourth band feat,
North Iowa's Festival Parade of Bands
(With all the pomp and skill that each
      commands).
The "Music Man" is imaged here
And River City is the sphere
Of Meredith Willson's Legend—we avow,
A music-making legend to endow
A world of student musicmen
With laughter, song and fame—so, then
We *welcome you* to River City *now!*

IOWA THE TALL

Music by Robert Logan, Clear Lake
Words by Mary Wilcox

Iowa the tall—
Iowa, where tall men tower,
Reap the wealth and the power of the land,
Iowa shall stand
Iowa the tall.
Tawny waves are growing, glowing;
Iowa is the grandest state of all—
Iowa is tall!

Oh, rocketing grain, harvest unfurled,
Bounty of industry, hope for the world
Bred Iowa tall——spread Iowa wide.
Oh, the Lord built our land strong in prairie
        pride!

Iowa is heart . . .
And the glory of our nation.
Great the name where the halls of learning
Chart the forward state
So that Iowa will always tower tall.

THE AUTHOR

Mary Wilcox, born in Sioux City, Iowa, and educated in Duluth, Minn., is a resident of Mason City, Iowa. She is a wife and mother . . . and between household tasks and her radio interview work, Mrs. Wilcox writes poetry and prose. For her regular radio interview programs, she promotes cityman-farmer cooperation and emphasizes the role of woman in modern society. She interviews local community leaders and national personalities—to tell the story of "Iowa the Tall."

ARTIST ON FEDERAL AVENUE

(To the best Display Artist in Iowa—my husband, Leo)

Cosmopolitan aura in window display,
Manikins garbed in stylish array
Image finesse and fashion sense prone
To the cultural state where tall talent is grown.

COVER JACKET DESIGN
BY LEO WILCOX

AL MARTIN

INSIDE ILLUSTRATIONS
BY AL MARTIN, MASON CITY